The Thought Power

OrangeBooks Publication

Smriti Nagar, Bhilai, Chhattisgarh - 490020

Website: **www.orangebooks.in**

First Edition, 2022

ISBN: 978-93-5621-032-5

Know How to Make Your Life Beautiful

The Thought Power

by Madhav Varadi

OrangeBooks Publication

www.orangebooks.in

Acknowledgements

My sincere Thanks to you the Reader for choosing this book to know the "The Thought Power".

I'm very grateful to my spiritual masters who always teach something new about the multiple shades of life. To my parents and my grandparents who always been with me and supported me every time.

Our Masters are someone who made this possible and always encourage us to be tough in following the truthful ways in our life.

My Mother is somcone who always backed me in every step, who gave me the motivation to not give up easily on anything. Our Love is simple yet unconditional.

My Father is my true inspiration. He always encouraged me in my life to do better every time and who taught me that nothing comes easier and nothing stays permanent.

My smiling Grandfather who always have a smile in his face. I never saw him lost his temper how worse the situation been and that teach me many things. He is someone who finds happiness everywhere and that inspire m e the most.

My special gratitude to my friends and my relatives with whom I make better times, these are who supports me and who are in the beautiful times of life with me.

Finally, My heart full of love and gratitude to my Life for having the greatest masters to teach and support me in living, to have all these people around me and for the different experiences I experience. I Love my life and I Thank to have what I deserve.

Sometimes it is just a small thought to raise a Hope to never give up easily on anything we desire to have in our life.

Index

Introduction

"The Thought Power" is something which is to tell the power of your own thinking and your own thoughts. The thoughts which can bring the glory you are missing or which you always wanted to have in your life. It is to bring the change from your sadness and to keep you moving with the knowledge of positivity from your own thoughts. This is something which doesn't tell you anything beyond this world but the basic things which can show major impacts in your life if you make them your daily routine. This book is to tell you about some important things which can bring you happiness and to spread happiness in everyone. To make positivity from what you do. It is because at the end of the day, it is only our happiness and the happy faces we create are that matters to our head even how hard we spend the complete day.

Have you ever observed how your own thoughts and how your own thinking make the way in your daily life? Haven't you observed how your thoughts change your mood and the mood changing your whole situation? YES!!!.....they do!! That usually happens because everything works with our own thoughts in our life. They keep on moving us every day as we think. We Think, We Work, We Become..... Now you may think that, I am not living a life which I never thought or dreamt of but actually you are living this life because you thought it to be like this at a certain time. If you are sad- the things around you will be messing you, if you are happy- how worst the situation be you will find a source to laugh later. This may not happen quicker but definitely happen and that is what the power of the thinking is and it will happen because that is how it is designed to work. The more worse you think about your situation, the more worse your chances in different situations of your life will be and will become. The more positive and happy you are now, you will always find a way to get out of any type of critical situation you are facing and bring happiness.

We can only specify the difference between the positive and negative by the knowledge we have in time and situations. Our knowledge & experiences in this cycle of life will tell us everything about how we are going to spend our remaining life. The things which we often don't care will sometime have major impacts and which we care much may have nothing. Everything that is happening around us will definitely direct us to the destination of our life which may result to a good side or a bad side. Learning is the biggest thing which will teach us many new lessons and will show the purpose and the meaning of our life. Life is about understanding every situation and moving without any limits. It doesn't have any boundaries and no one can stop you but your own thoughts can do. Don't let that happen and get more knowledge about the power of your thoughts to make that bring change in your life with happiness all around.

Think Bigger!!

The belief you have in yourself and in your attitude decide the next moves of your life. You are the only one who create your own destiny, then why you are wasting your time in thinking smaller. It maybe because of the fear or doubt you have in yourself. Fear not for anything and always aim bigger. That will show you the way to the destination of your life to the biggest. Never doubt in yourself, if your thoughts to become great are pure and true, your result will be definitely unpredictable. Not every time you win, also not every time you lose. You need to have patience and it will respond to your will power. Sometimes you win, sometimes you learn but you will never fail. The result which won't come as expected is not a failure. It is a lesson which will move us to succeed. It tells you to change your way. It answers you the questions that come in the way of success but it is not the end.

Confidence, patience, attitude and positivity play a major role in your path to succeed. Be kind to everyone. Be confident in yourself. Try to be more patient. Maintain good attitude everywhere. Every living being wants to be respected and everyone deserves respect. Treat animals kindly. Don't harm them for your happiness. Control your anger and be calm always. It brings you positivity, so does the happiness, so does the good result. Try to think from every person's point of view to make better judgements. Think bigger and nature will benefit you depending in your behaviour. Be positive and it will bring most of anything you want to have in your life.

There are many unknown truths we experience everyday but we doesn't know the complete impact of those facts. These things can bring major changes in our life and it will be in our thoughts to give them more preference after knowing about them. The things which can have major impact in our life are Gratitude, Love and Attitude. We discuss about them in this book and also define how they lay us a way in empowering our way to the success in our life influencing our thoughts. We talk about the power of our thinking which can change the complete way of our living and which will show a new way in our life from now if we follow the knowledge that is been shared from this book, "The Thought Power".

Now, after we came to know that our thoughts are the main reason behind changing our lives and how effective they are in bringing everything to us, we think and give a chance in changing our thinking to be positive every time but it doesn't happen that simple because without knowing about how to bring positive vibes around us in any situation how can we change our thoughts. Even that happened for now it won't stay long as I told bringing positivity needs changing thoughts and depends completely in the knowledge which we hold longer. The knowledge we have takes us to the different experiences in our lives. It is very important to always stay in the loyal side and let other things work frequently depending on it. This book is to share the different experiences which everyone can have after knowing the knowledge of the thought power and how it shape peace and happiness in the people who think they only have sadness in their life. It is to bring positivity in everyone and bring the importance of being grateful for every matter we are living in this land.

As you keep on going through this book you will come to know the different things which are small without its knowledge but can bring larger changes in your life if you heart fully intend to love and be grateful for everything, everyone you have and the joy in your life, to use your complete "Thought Power" to bring what you desired in your life.

Prologue

There will never be anything if you haven't given something in return to get what you want. What is the thing you want to give to get what you wanted? What do you really wanted to have in your life? And it decides and makes you how much you need to give. Moreover it's just your time and thoughts which you need to invest in your dreams. The most powerful your thoughts are, the most pleasant your life will be. Spending your time in dreaming is not a bad idea but you needed to visualize everything clearly is what matters the most. You need to have a clear vision about where you wanted to grow tomorrow will bring the only hope that makes you stand far from most of the people who give up ending on something which they never expect to come in their life.

The best part of the life which anyone can have is the capability of understanding the things that are going in our life. Our fate is never decided by God or Deity, it is our own thoughts which influence us to be like what we desired. Relating to many of the experiments, there are actually thousands of things that run in a human mind every hour. The main thing here is that those thousands of thoughts should relate to one thing and that should be your dream. And now it is the only thing to keep in your mind that we should not let anything behind our dreams to come in our mind. Being cautious of our own thoughts already brings most part of the success we want to have in our life.

Focussing on one thing is never an easy condition with having many things running in our mind but we need to keep on shifting them to only one and that is our target to reach in our life. The more confidence you have in yourself, the most powerful your thoughts work in shaping your future. Manifestations are never wrong and also result depends upon the process we go through. Stop listening to the people or words who never been in your situation and whose only work is to keep on talking and judging about others.

Never in your life let words influence against your heart. There's always something between your heart and mind. As the mind thinks so as the heart needs to follow but sometimes there will be many things which our heart doesn't like to have in our life. Shaping both heart and mind in one thing is also never an easy task. If they both get to be in same way then you'll be unstoppable in getting what you always deserve.

How Attraction Works!!

What actually Attraction means? Is this Newton's law of attraction? YES, it is…!! It is Newton's third law which say, "For every action there's always an equal and opposite reaction". Now don't think you have to give millions to get millions. The millions you have to spend are your thoughts. The more powerful your thoughts are, the more effective they work.

To keep progress you always need to hustle, you should never think against your will power or against what you desired. One needed to bring all the forces which are behind you to receive what you wanted. The people who are always stronger without losing hope, to them everything co-operates- the nature, the body, the people, mostly the mind.

Our minds are interconnected with the nature, so as our thoughts, so as our surroundings will become. One doesn't need to give everything for what they desire, though it depends on the things which one dreamed or needed. Most of the people spend their time in searching for a good partner to share their life or to bring happiness in their lives. The thing here is sometimes being Alone is actually a blessing. Loneliness is never a negativity which disturbs your life rather it's your thoughts who think that brings negativity. Being alone filters the best to come out of your life and make you choose what you truly want in your life. It's your own thoughts which bring every change in your life, let it be about belief, wealth, people, happiness, sadness etc.

Life doesn't have rules to make it go following a certain pattern. Life is meant to be followed as your heart desire. Be crazier! Does that really affect your life? Neverthless you think it does affect until it don't. The more pressure you keep on your mind, the more effective your mind works. Maybe there are also chances in showing negative impacts on your lives. Sometimes you need to slow down the pace to let your engines work properly. Always pressurizing mind may also have negative impact on your life.

For example, if hard work is the only option to become rich there should never be a labour who really works harder from waking to sleeping. What most of the successful people have and what all these people don't have is the ideas and thoughts about how to dream of something and make it to come real. It's never late if you get married at your 30's or its never early if you invest in your 20's. Follow your own rules and create your own path. Spend most of your time with yourself to work on things which your life wants to live. Spending time with yourself brings or tells what your life wants and your heart will surely show you a way to get to that living. Many things will have impact on your life. Happiness or sadness doesn't come simply as they wanted to, they do come depending on your actions.

The way you behave with other people brings the same to you. You give love, you get. You give money, you get. You give time, you get. For everything you give you will get multiple of it but the same happens with negativity also. You make sad someone, you get. You spread fear in someone, you get. You feel jealous or awkward about someone, you get. Negative or Positive will definitely return to you because that is how the nature works which is, 'You get what you give'.

* * *

Thoughts, thoughts, thoughts…. These are the biggest things in everyone's lives. One should never underestimate their own selves when they're in any work or situation. There are always two results after completing any work - one is to win and other is to learn. Enjoy the process of your work and it brings happiness to you even you didn't get what you wanted to get as its result. You may keep on failing many times but one day you will definitely win and these failures make you a way to win finding different solutions to the upcoming questions in your success. Finally you win, not just with your confidence but because there are no options for you to lose. You will win because there are lot of answers with you in every direction the questions about your success arise. Our mindset is the most important thing which will have a major impact in our lives. It is not the people or the atmosphere which brings the change in the situations, it is our own thoughts which are most powerful in lightening our life or to bring it to the dark.

Every living being have different thoughts and everyone wants to live it to the fullest. If you start to think about happiness, everything around you looks happier. If you think about sadness even winning a jackpot brings you mourning. And in happiness even if you lose anything, it will direct you to give that an another try until you win. Happiness and sadness are just a part of a life then why wasting time hanging around them. Bring smiles in the faces of people beside you but never cries or sadness.

Attracting happiness brings positivity without knowing and attracting sadness brings negativity. Choose wisely what you want and how your life wanted to be. Don't hang with something that hurt or irritate you. Leave behind those thoughts which affect your mind. Change your mind to choose happiness over sadness. Spread love, spread laugh- you may not get result soon but you will get when your time needed.

No one in this earth want to spoil their lives, it's just the situations and the time which changes everything in just a fraction of seconds. Never judge too soon or without knowing about anything completely. Never believe anyone quickly or be one sided without knowing what happened from the other side. Life is not meant for fights, argues, sadness, heart breaks etc. Life is meant to have fun all the time- love, happiness, enjoyments etc., are what needed to live a peaceful life and make it worthy. Everything comes and goes with the power of our thoughts, choose wisely every time what your life is meant to have all around with you.

Be kind, be loyal, give respect, give love, don't variate the people with relations and among the relations. Everyone have hearts and everyone have the feelings. Don't lose your character for the bad things. Be hard, be tough for the things you always want to have in your life. Never back down for anything if one's you decided to have something heart fully for you. Your confidence, attitude and behaviour are the important things for every variation's you choose to have in your life. Don't expect anything in return for what you do now. You will receive what you deserve depending on your process of behaving and your thoughts. Don't depend in anyone completely and make your life fill your dreams with your own pockets and the knowledge.

Learning is the main thing in every process. You will never fail in anything if you start learning from the process you choose to have success in. You are always a step behind your success if you choose failure and a step ahead of your success if you choose learning. Because choosing failure brings regret and stops you from pushing forward but learning bring new methods in achieving success and it'll keep you ahead of your success. Learning is really a biggest thing- let it be about people, situations, processes etc. Keep on learning something new making a way to gain knowledge and open your mind doors to attain good things. Spend time with your elders, wise people or if you can't do that spend time reading books to get knowledge and new experiences.

Reading is a greatest hobby which no one teaches you to make it a habit because no one ever tries it to be a habit beyond many things. Knowledge is what needed to handle any type of situations and if you handle situations listening from unwise people, no one ever tries you to choose to handle situations. You get the wisest knowledge listening to the wise people and they mostly share them with the books. You can also learn those things from your gadgets but books are really a fantastic making which make you feel some positive type of vibe in getting knowledge. Carrying a book always feed your mind and your attitude with a different way of living. Here, reading is not about the academic books or job bringing books rather the books which talk about life, which brings you hope, which show you a way to move forward with the knowledge it brings to you, which get answers to the questions you want to get answered in your life.

Be conscious every time and you'll get most of the answers to the questions which you want to be answered. Observe everything around you carefully. Focus on the actions and movements in everything around you carefully. Nature brings you peace and it's just enough to have everything which you want to experience in your life. It shows you different shades depending on your interaction with the nature. The water, the air, the food, the soil etc., all comes under nature and it's also the thing which brings whatever we want to experience in our life. Respect everything and everyone. Understand situations completely before starting any interaction to suggest or argue in between any situation someone facing.

Try to think from the other side of you when talking with people. Among the billions of people you are not the only one who has the heart and feelings in it. Everyone wants respect to be given and their emotions also matter to them the most. So, it's better to not hurt someone without knowing anything completely. To all the living beings there exist the same feelings. Not rich, not poor everyone wants to be loved and cared. It's just the change of behaviour and attitude with the incomes but the emotions between hearts are equal for all. Mostly for middle class people, they work hard to gain a good name in the society and that shouldn't be gone easily with just your mistake for disrespecting them in public. Anger makes people foolish, when anger takes over calmness, our mind won't be in our control and there starts everything which makes larger impacts. Try not to get angry without knowing anything completely rather push yourself to convert the anger into finishing any work. Use your anger on yourself that why aren't you able to complete any given work faster? Turn your anger into positivity, to push yourself forward which can bring you confidence and direct you to the way through which you want to settle in your life.

Life is all about creating chances, chances to change our future, the chances to make our future. See future through those chances you are creating. It shows you the way to your destination. Keep on learning from everything, you still have lots of space in your brain to store any large data's you want to store. Use them according to the situation which comes under you to get handled. Be conscious to observe everything around you- in people, in nature, in situations. Gain lots of knowledge that you will be able to handle any type of situations with ease without making things complex and time taking. Don't doubt the capacity of your brain, it have enough space for everything which you want to get stored. We humans have larger storage capacities in our brain that it can store any type of data but we doesn't use it to the fullest and also mourn for the same thing without knowing it's capacity. Your largest and biggest dreams show you the way to your success and everything around you will be changing according to it. Fear not for the changes around you. Be brave to handle any type of situations. Aim bigger and you will know the worth of your life.

Thoughts on life needs:

In every human life the important things are food, water and shelter. These are the most essential things for every human being and they can do anything to get these for their living. There are also many people who are working only for food and not for any specific needs. Food is something which binds all the people irrespective of any region. So, Food is the biggest need for everyone. Your thoughts on food also describe it to be in favourable to you or to be opposite to you.

In ancient days there was a better understanding between people like if they share what their crop is they would have get other crop for its worth and they used to get all their essentials of food with crop for crop. Now with raising population and different sectors in works and jobs the demand to crop for crop has been reduced (may also happening now in small places) and the use of money became vastly important in every human life. Without money there is nothing became the situation these days. And money comes to the one who are capable of earning it. To earn money you have to work. To get anything you need, you have to give anything. You give your energy and time, so it turns into money. Money is ruling all the world and those who has lots of money are the rulers of the world. You may not think about ruling the world but at least you may have a dream of ruling your own house. To rule people with whom you have bond with, you need to fulfil their wishes and you have to buy them what they needed. Again, here you need money to get what they need. So, you need to learn things about how to get money and to balance it to rule your own house. Money gets you and your family most of the things needed but you need to use it effectively to simply not waste it for unnecessary things and also need to learn saving it to not ask for a helping hand when its necessary is very important.

Now we get to know that the most efficient one's which can show a major impact in everyone's life are our own thoughts. Positive thoughts keep us happy and the negative thoughts keep us unhappy. Change your thinking and see the difference with your eyes. It brings you peace and it brings you victory. Don't doubt on this thing. Believe and rest happens with the flow as you deserve. Make right moves thinking of all the consequences of good and bad before doing anything. One's decision made stand tall to your plans without thinking further more about anything. Some decisions may affect others, so think about your next moves carefully and move according to your plans without affecting anyone. There will be options for anything if we concentrate to fix the things. Make options to match with the needs you want to have in your way to success. Don't hurt anyone and carry the burden with you wherever you go.

Making Focus:

Train yourself to deal with the people. Train your body to be in your control to fit for any type of situations. Train your mind not to lose its calm in however the situation will be. Be independent and believe in your ideas to make them work. In the same way never disappoint the one who is dependent in you. Take care of all the things that happen around you which ask your presence. Also don't be present in any type of situation where you or your people don't get any attention. Mind your own business so that you can build or create what your heart desires.

For all the things that are happening around us, it's our own fate which we created to take place. It's never late to start things right now, don't get disappoint for past or the things which are not going as planned. Change the process and keep on changing till you get your result. Don't keep more doubts about yourself on your worth. Don't mess your mind. It's always not necessary to follow the routine daily things. Take break. Be crazy. Hang out for peace. At the end it's only your happiness you needed the most. Don't work to convince others or change your plans for others. You, yourself have a great partner within you. Spend time with yourself and you'll bring the best out of you.

Change your thoughts to aim bigger, to think bigger. Surround yourself with the people who always have lots of positivity and who keep on pushing you that you are able to do and you will get what you wanted. Don't surround yourself with people who discourage you even you make things happier for them. Our thoughts describe how our surroundings will be, always think large to get larger.

It is impossible to focus on only one thing in our complete time of a day until that becomes true. But the thing is you need to be positive in whatever your thinking is going along. Let there be many thoughts running in your mind but that should give you spirit to move further happily and build confidence. Your thoughts should not affect you to lose belief and change your whole mood to negativity. That'll not only mess with the present but also changes the future. So, it is always necessary to be positive or at least try to come back faster from negative situations to not make it show much effect further in your life.

It is always easier to tell someone to follow principles for maintaining a good balance in life. But what I think is the correct right to tell principles to others should be the one who actually follows them. One can't teach you any subject without having any knowledge in it. It is important to follow someone after knowing what they have experienced with that. In the same way it is also good to follow new things but the emotions and the challenges will be different. If you are stuck in between following the new one or the experienced one, listen to your heart and follow it, that always choose the best to stay with you. Whatever happens, it will be just an experience which stays now. How happy or sad it may be it is only staying now. You can't have it in the future or even had, it won't surprise you as happened now. Nothing stays permanent - people, wealth, happiness and sadness or even us. It is all a part of this planet and it all recreates everything.

It is not good to make others sacrifice anything or to make their happiness lose for us. As we have our own thoughts about our life, everyone have thoughts about theirs too. So, let's respect everyone's and try to fulfil them or at least try to not make them gets disturbed with our activities. It is always good to think something beyond our own limits and also from other shoes to know the worth of something in their life. If we know our thoughts will be effective in creating everything around us, never choose to dominate the one who helps you to do your work or choose to dominate any other people. They may work under you or you are giving shelter to them, it doesn't mean they need to be like slaves under you and give their life to you. Be in there position and think what you had preferred if you were in that place and start moving to make things convenient to them. As nothing stays permanent don't let bad knowledge be spread to your coming future generations. Be an example to bring Spirit in them but not to get vanished in the name of something bad. This is necessary to discuss all this, because our mind never makes us to be calm. Even you control, the situations around you won't let that calmness stay strong. So, think affectively before choosing what you want in your life. We can do anything with our thought power and it all need is some positive and better time.

So, as the thoughts make everything that is happening around us, it is important for everyone to have peace all the time. To bring positivity in every situation we need to have peaceful mind and it comes making our atmosphere friendly to us in return. To make it friendly, we first need to begin with bringing changes in the way we deal with everyone & everything. It is not a big task to make that because we are now going to show love & gratitude to everyone which brings us the same in return. So, to bring changes in others it is necessary to bring change in ourselves so that everything around us will change. Now, we will be going to discuss briefly about how we are going to make love & gratitude work effectively in our life in the next chapters.

Gratitude

Have you ever heard the word Gratitude before? Do you really know what its importance is? How it shows impact in our behaviour to change our thoughts? Okay!! Let's start with introducing Gratitude clearly. If you already know about it, let you just try to know about it better or if you doesn't 't know what Gratitude is, let you try to start knowing about Gratitude from here now completely. In simple Gratitude is being Thankful. Thankful truly from heart for everything and everyone and every situation we go through our whole day.

Being Thankful to something or someone has never been a biggest thing in many of our lives. Showing Gratitude to all the creation that will involve in our daily life is like showing them their importance for us. Here Creation involves people, food, water, nature, daily needs etc., Now, you may think what all this is about? But, when we go in detailed to this gratitude thing it shows a lot of impact in them and also within us if we try to change things using Gratitude. It vanishes most of the sorrows we get and also makes us not to lose our control when we are alone or in group of people who are messing our heads.

Humans spend most of their time in always expecting something which isn't present in their life. We spend our time to get those things which we wanted to have in our life and also work for the same. In search of those things most of the people finally end with lots of regret in their life if they're unable to get what they desired. Life is all about the chances we create to get what we desire but in the same way we should also respect many of the things which are already present in our life. Being Grateful to whatever come or go in life is one of the important things which most of the people doesn't know. Gratitude plays a major role in everyone's life letting them get most of the needs humans desire to have in their life.

Being grateful releases proud feelings or disrespect over other people. It convinces someone easily that nothing is received simply but with some effort to get what we wanted. In our way of achieving something, we often forget many things or people who support us and finally when we get what we desired there maybe chances that we totally forget to care about them. And hence we change the people who support us to the people who want us to fail. This change not only happens with the people but also with many things that get involved in our day-to-day life which impacts our life.

We humans are always busy in searching many things which we don't have right now. But in search of those things we should not lose those things which we already have in our lives. Not giving chances to lose something and also to receive many things which we desired, being Grateful to all the things which exist and which are going to exist is a biggest reality in one's life. Yes! So that is what gratitude can do. It can do that because gratitude is filled with your emotions. You can't be thankful to any creation if you have negative feelings for them. Thanksgiving only happens when you are true from your heart and that is where everything starts from. When you are true for something you do, you not only win that, also there's most of the chance to make it bring positivity around you. The positivity you get will further change your future bringing better thoughts in you.

As you observe carefully your life is far more better than most of the lives that exist in this planet. First of all starting with our body - Do you show respect to your body which always co-operates as you wish? If you don't do, it's never too late to start it from now and you'll observe the difference you get in your life after you start practising this gratitude exercise. There are some daily routines in gratitude exercise which will become effective in your daily life if you start following them.

> The first thing to start your fresh morning is to be grateful that you are alive today and you are not amongst most of the people who left their lives. Say, Thank You that I'm alive today and today will be a great day for me with lots of happiness and also whatever comes let it come and whatever goes let it go.

> The second thing to be grateful for is to your body, the temple of your life. Our body is like temple of our life which should always be kept clean and to take more care. Say, Thank You to my body for always co-operating with me as I want you.

> The important thing to be grateful for is to the food which we eat, which gives us energy to do whatever we want every time. Most of the people feel bad that they don't have different recipes on their table. But the thing is that most of the people don't even have what you are getting to eat. Let it just be a handful of Rice you get and you are not among the people who spend their days with empty stomachs.

➤ Not just regarding food there are many things in our lives to which we should always be grateful. Never think that you don't have anything in your life or you are unlucky to born like this or that. Whatever you have now is far much better than most of the population. Let you have a friend or relative or colleague to ask whether you had a good day or not is better than being alone without anyone to take care of your life.

➤ Besides we should be very grateful to the water which brings lots of energy and difference in our body. We can live without food but not without water. It's a main source for everything. Water does many works to us every day, from waking to sleeping it's rare that in a gap of an hour there's no involvement of water. We should show gratitude to water whenever we use it for any purpose in our life. From drinking to bathing or washing we must have gratitude to water, for the peace it gives to our inner senses. Without water there's nothing remained in our lives or in this planet, Earth. One must never forget to pray or at least show gratitude to the water for being a main source of our breaths.

Since there are many things in everyone's day to day lives regarding one's individual daily routines, be grateful for all those things and people who bring both sadness and happiness to your life. Now don't be in a dilemma that is it okay to also be grateful for sadness. Most of our daily life basis depends upon our past actions. What we are today is because how we were yesterday and how we are today decides our tomorrow. That's how actually our lives are designed to work. What we are going through our daily life is a part of our actions of yesterday. So it is important to accept sadness or happiness because nothing stays permanent. This only stays now but we react more to the sadness and keep it with us to make it more important and let it change all the happiest situations too. We take sadness from it and impact it in happy situations and thus create negativity. The same happens with the happy situations but you take happiness from here and it builds positivity.

Taking care of our present both in handling people and situations will bring much difference to our Future. It's always okay to start something new now without feeling regret that it would be good if I had started something before. It's never late to realize things which are made to show impact in our lives. Never feel bad for how your past was, at least try to change your future by convincing your present. Try not to involve more in arguments or most of the things which hurt others feelings. Because the more intensity you create in your surroundings the more impact it shows whether positively or negatively. It is not easy to gain lots of support from everyone quickly but one small incident is enough to create the trauma around you. That is why it is important to be conscious every time to know what is happening with you.

Coming to the gratitude exercise, I call it as an exercise because one should not forget it in any type of situation. Like food and like water necessary every day, gratitude also needed to be given importance. The Love you show through gratitude towards others makes those relations stay stronger. So, it isn't just something we avoid like most of the things we avoid in our life, it have real impact and it is important. Let think some of the important common creations and note down all the things which play a role in your daily life. Most of the common things in every human's life to be grateful for are:

1. God

2. Parents or who takes care of you

3. Body

4. Nature

5. Machines

6. People

7. Money

8. Properties... etc, if you have any other add them.

We should be detailed in showing gratitude for something which we wanted to be grateful for. The more detailed we are, the more convincing it will be for whom we are being grateful... For example, Thank you Water for always taking care of the people who are depended in you. So, let's try this for those common things which are present in everyone's life,

1. Thank you God for your creation and my life.

2. Thank you to my Mom and Dad and my siblings for your true love.

3. Thank you to my Body for always co-operating as I wanted and for the good health I have.

4. Thank you to this beautiful Nature for always showing something attracting and also thank you to the air which I breathe.

5. Thank you to all my machines and electronic gadgets.

6. Thank you to the people who are involved in my today's life.

7. Thank you to the money which I have and which I'm receiving.

8. Thank you to all the properties which I own and which I'm going to own.

To all these above lines you can add more things depending in your daily life structure to which you think to be grateful for. The detailed saying of gratitude for something will create a positive vibe inside you and show their importance to you whenever you hear about that. It'll be good to you if you recall all these at least twice a day; when you wake up in the morning and when you will go to sleep in the night. You keep on being grateful for all those things which impact your daily life. For every new change we wish to bring in our life, it takes a minimum of 21 days to make it a habit and a maximum of 41 days. So, give it a try and see what change it'll bring to your future comparing your present.

If you are unable to add emotion to anything, think their absence in your life and it will definitely create the impact. For example, take food- now think what your situation will be if you are not able to feed your stomach every day. Just thinking about it only show a lots of importance for food, so it adds the emotion if you are unable to add on anything that is important or involved in your daily life.

The money and the time are the important assets in every human life. You need to know how to spend them properly to not make them suffer you. Time and money are different yet their importance is high in world. If you play with time and money without any purpose they also do the same when there need is important to you.

Time is something which never comes again one's gone. Most of the people don't value the time in present but feel for it when it becomes past. One's gone is gone. It won't repeats now, so don't feel to what has happened, learn from it and make your present better. It will eventually change your future which will bring you the positivity helping you to grow your thoughts in your life.

The true value of money comes to those who struggle, who work hard and know its complete worth. There are many people who spend lots of money when they have it and also feel to think saving it the before. Money is something which is completely ruling the modern world. There are many stories who gave their lives for money and also many relations which broke for money. Don't become one of them and know the true worth of something to really make it work for you. Be grateful for what you have. Use Gratitude when there is the purpose of money. Tell money to get returned to you the multiple times and be grateful to it whole heartedly whenever you use it.

Gratitude really helps you to grow in your life and also as a person. It shows you the real value of everything you have in your life and also to which you wish to have in our life. Use visualization clearly and have a good vision of your dreams. Don't spoil your energy for bad things which affect you and the people around you, rather use it to make everyone around you happy. You can't be thinking opposite to what a real human is and wish to have all the pleasures. You need to be true from your heart that you won't be affecting anyone and any creation in this nature. Fight with yourself to become a true real man than fighting with others to be opposite to that. Replace your complaints with gratitude and it brings the change you wish into your life.

A real human is someone who values everything which they have. They will always be grateful for whatever they have in their life. They respect everyone, everything and have love to every creation in the world. The truthfulness they follow brings them a good character, a great attitude and a lot of braveness. They will have knowledge to differentiate good things and bad things. They always find happiness in whatever they do and they will be heart full in doing any work given to them. They make positivity and spread peace around them so it brings them positive atmosphere. Nature encourages them in what they do helping to make them succeed in their work. These are the people who build what they want. Try to be someone real and change your mind to reach your goal.

My Experience:

I believe gratitude this much because I have experienced this bringing the change in my life. When I didn't know gratitude I had many things which were disturbing me. I had everything to eat but no happiness in it, also I used to have arguments with my parents at least twice a week. I had some money issues and I wasn't finding peace whatever I do. I was totally messing with my life and I wasn't happy with what I was going through. I had many friends to spend happy times but I was all alone. I was completely in search of the peace I wanted in my life so I finally came to know about Gratitude through a book and that changed me everything. After that I saw people who were in search of peace more badly than I wanted, so I liked to share the power of our thoughts which can change our whole life.

It is most common in the people of growing age to feel the different shades of life. I never knew what this life thing was, why we get birth and death, why do we need to struggle this much if we are going to die definitely. There were many unanswered questions in my life which made me nothing to do. I was desperately in search of those answers to know what all this is about. What I only remembered mostly was to not stop anywhere and to keep on moving whatever it will be. I later got many experiences which changed my mind but the questions will be keeping on rising with new experiences.

I observed this not only in me but also in many of the people who had known anything about life. It is because of the knowledge of life we have in that growing ages, probably between 15 to 23 years in most of the people. Different emotions, different thoughts, different experiences and everything use to look different if happened first time. Sometimes even happen again it may teach something new. So there is something which is common in most of the people and that is Hope. We don't know what will happen tomorrow but we plan for the next day. It is giving the hopes to not stop where we are stuck in, actually we won't stop anywhere. Whatever it may be, we will definitely move forward how good or bad the situation might be. It is the only mantra to live a good life that is to keep pace of life and the experiences teaches us many of our unanswered questions.

It is not that simple as we just talk about anything. It needs determination to just move with hope in life. If you don't have belief that you are not going to change your life, you will be in those conditions only which keep you in between negativities. You need to question your life about your situation and you should be desperate to change it. My thoughts were so badly in search of peace that time so that made me find gratitude, later I also got the knowledge in making our dreams come true through our thoughts. So, it is totally our thoughts which change our life. The desperation we have will show us the way and change everything. We simply don't spend our whole day for work if we are not willing to work. It is our thought which is making us to work the whole day. It is your thoughts if you find this book and get to know all this knowledge of how to change your life.

I was all in awestruck when I found those changes after making Gratitude & Love a habit. I was happy with whatever I had and I was getting many things I wanted to have in my life. I hardly remember when I had arguments with my parents. I found happiness in whatever I eat and I'm now completely free from money issues. I had found peace even I was alone and it was actually making me better every day. I spent most of my time with myself and I had peace in everything I do. I'm all grown up now from a position where I was upset with my life to getting happiness from wherever I wanted to have and whatever I do. I totally use my thought power and I'm grateful for this life I'm living. I learnt to make positivity and it brings the same to me in most of the situations I go through. Sometimes it acts different but I need to move to know what it is going to teach me this time.

Being Grateful will be like a blessing if you get attached to the gratitude exercise for everything that's happening in your daily life and without your presence of understanding you'll be able to watch miracles happen in your Life. It's happiness which is missing in many of the people. Even they have most of the things which many of the people doesn't have they still find peace in them. So, it is not about material things bringing happiness, it should be finding happiness in mostly everything and gratitude helps you in bringing something you are missing. I'm a true example of this exercise and also you'll be one among them to taste the magic of gratitude. It doesn't take your hours of time, it just takes some of your time but you needed to do it heart fully. Always remember one thing 'whatever is happening now, will only stay now'. When you go to bed in the night you should needed to be able to leave all those things which weren't your way and should use which were your way to bring positivity in you. You will be able to make a whole day good with your better starts in the morning. So, it is very important to always start your day with fresh mornings, with positivity, with some better ray of hope than yesterday towards your goal.

Follow your own set of rules and get attached to it sincerely. Create your own path to live and also don't let any situation change those rules. Some days may get altered but they shouldn't change all the way. Set your mind to be in your space and don't let anything from outside change your thinking. As you think, you work. As you work, you will become.

* * *

Life is a very unpredictable thing, you predict one there happens something different, you think to have different there happens something another. But you should always have hope in your dreams that you'll definitely get what you wanted to have in your life. Things or situations may go unpredictable but what about the dreams. One surely needed to have clear and complete belief in them that "One day I'm going to have this", if you are true for what you desired and if you are courageous to not give up on your dreams in any chances, you are going to reach that. The process may change with the work you are doing or the time may change but if you are patient and confident in yourself being true, you'll conquer your thought one day.

Everything is going to be tested in this process; your behaviour, belief, patience, confidence, attitude and everything will be on the desk and also you may be completely exhausted with whatever you are doing and lost all your hope. And there starts everything many of the times. It is never easy to get what you dreamt of, it takes lot of your thinking about someone, the character you have, the love and passion you have to become successful. Every successful person may have definitely gone through many shades of the life which only they remember. It is not as simple as we just talk about someone's success. One needed to have complete grit on themselves to go through all the different shades of life. No one can expect what happens tomorrow, so it is all gratitude and love which keeps us moving with the positivity from everything we experience of yesterday's and march us in the present.

It is always necessary to do work heart fully. That only brings joy in whatever you do and keep you focussed more in the work. Most of the people I seen do their work not because they love it or they want it, they just do it like they doesn't have any chances left in their life. Those will be the people who are not able to dare or lost confidence in themselves. One needed to always remember one thing that, wherever you find happiness you should be present there. You dream one and you do one. Why? Question yourself and if you think what you are doing now is correct that may be because of the situations you were in. But it doesn't happen with everyone. Most of the people quit in middle without facing the real flavour of life. The more harder the chances become, the more closer you will be to get what you had desired. Your way is becoming tough because of the strength your dream has. Enjoy the process, it may take lot of time but you need to have patience to reach your dream.

Love everything. Love the tougher situation either for trying you. No one preferably go till there, be happy that you are going to experience it. Don't think about result, it depends in what you had gone through your life. But at present enjoy the process you are facing. Learn everything what it is going to teach you that it'll help you if u had failed or even passed don't forget the experiences you gone through.

No one wants to know the process you were going through, they just needed your result. Then why do you want to care about what they talk about you. You can't guarantee that they'll think that you have succeeded because of your hard work. They'll talk whatever you do and that just happens because that is how the success is built. The more gossips you listen the more strong you become and it happens if you choose them in a right way to build yourself else it'll be the one which will completely reverse your entire situation. Your consciousness is very important in every aspect of your life. Let all these things be aside of you, let them talk whatever they want to talk because they're not the one who feed people around you. It'll be only you who knew what you went through and also it'll be only you who know the complete value of everything you have in your life. You are the true person to enjoy your success and it is the result to the struggle you had in your life.

Don't stop moving forward but it eventually won't stop either. Always remember to be kind and spread much love as possible. If you take this life thing harder, it will look harder everywhere. If you take this easier, it will look easier everywhere. But both of them will have their consequences in your life. So, just try to keep everything simpler and go with the flow of your life. Be Grateful for the life you are living and just rock it with your "Thought Power".

Love

Love is a beautiful feeling, a magical essence in all the emotions, a wonderful creation in the universe. However described it gets well suited to the meaning of Love. It is neither been destroyed nor created easily without anyone's or anything interaction. If your love is true it'll definitely show you the way to get anything you given the love for. Love is a very sensitive feeling that it can be built or broke within short durations. But in many relations if the same love is true and stronger it can never be destroyed. Simply it is the main reason for many of the relations which are stronger till date.

Is Love only for the living beings? No, it is not. Love is not only meant for the people or the animals individually. It can be between anything and anyone in the universe. In every human being's life, there exist many people, animals, things, machines etc., mean even you won't own them, the love is same for all. It doesn't have any differences between. For all those with whom we interact mostly, the feeling Love can be shared. Don't think machines or things or Nature doesn't have emotions to show it back to you. They will be effective even they don't have life if you observe the difference before and after giving love to them. One's you start giving love to everything that's happening and involving in your daily life, you get a great feeling in yourself which bring lots of belief and strength to you upon yourself and it makes you to feel better that you are not alone and you have many things who take care of you daily and love you the same as you do when you start spreading love among everything.

It is only love which has lots of power to hold any type of relation between any two creations. Love is the only thing which keeps you high if you start giving it to others. If you have a feeling to spread love among all, it will be the only thing which can change your complete life totally to the way you have never destined to be. Most of the people feel sad if they don't find a lover for them, don't be upset for such things because you are lucky that you can spread love to anyone or anything you want to give. Love is never a relation between two people or two hearts, Love is a feeling between one person or one heart to all the remaining creations in the universe. From stars in the sky to the water drops in the land you can give love to everything and everyone. Why to end your life if you are not getting love from someone whom you wanted to get? Feel happy that you are not fallen in the wrong hands who doesn't have love for you. Never please someone to love you, you'll surely find someone who loves you to the fullest. Life will keep on giving you many opportunities to make it worthy but it's just your thoughts which don't use them for the good cause and end up in spoiling beautiful lives.

Most of the people always want Love from a person whom they love and in that process of finding who their true love is, many end up with regrets in life or many even ending their lives. One's you start changing your thoughts you will get clear information about what and how everything around you is going on and taking place. If you change your thoughts to stop finding love in someone you like and start caring about all the people or things that have so much of love for you, you may eventually end up getting the person you have been searching for.

If you start caring the people who love you, you will be the one who will make their life happier. Why feeling sad if someone is not accepting your love? You have many things which are giving lots of love to you, start caring those people and things such that your life will be a blessing and also they will feel a lot of happiness in their life because of you. One's you start thinking positive for all the things that may be anything that is happening around you, you will be the one to change your life to get peace and happiness all over your life. It's only your thoughts which make everything around you that you may get anything or lost anything, to love anything or to hate anything.

Love is Everything

Both the love and the hate are the emotions which can't be described easily, which have lots of impact in everyone's life. Love may take time to create but hate just take seconds to destroy all the relation. Love is a wonderful feeling that it can never be faked and also should not be faked. For the temporary happiness and satisfaction many people are choosing love to get pleasure and ending in spoiling life of other people. This all happens because of the chances we provide to everything. To get cheated or to cheat someone it's our own actions which create them. It's because of our own thoughts which make all these things to keep on moving around us whole life. To get good, one need to first think good and everything around them follows.

Showing love is never an easy task that too, to the things which we think won't show us love back is not an ordinary task. You need to change your thinking first to make it simple. You needed to start believing that you'll receive love from everything to which you will be giving love to and also to everyone you love.

A real example I can give is, sometimes I used to be frustrated with the situations which were around me. They spoil the whole mood and I don't want it to happen because it will have an impact in my future. So this was like whenever I get frustrated it used to change my whole mood and bring negative vibrations around me. This happens when I mostly had nothing to do. The loneliness sometimes plays with me badly. That again used to take me to worse times. I wanted to completely change that and turn it to work for me.

Time is also a very unpredictable thing, how it changes and how it moves is also not easier to understand. The world completely revolves under time and those who try to understand it will definitely understand about life clearly. Time changes the situations and it changes life. So it is important to have knowledge about every situation we will be going throughout our life. Experiences teaches many things and you need to use it when time changes.

So, I wanted to change all this and wanted to value my life than feeling lonely. Then I got the knowledge about loving and as usually I wanted to give it a chance. I used to love my situations and it kept on giving me different flavours of life. I got happiness in whatever I do and time also used to not keep me lonely many of the times. I used to find better alternatives to save my time and built positivity with the help of gratitude. That changed my atmosphere and it gave me confidence to deal with everything. I Love to be born as a human and I doesn't have to complain about anything. You can also be the one like me or better than me if you are more desperate to built positivity and change your life.

Giving Love is also the same exercise as we do with practicing the gratitude exercise. The things which involve in our daily life and for the people who have impact in our life, we give love for them. It will have your complete heart and if you act in this you will also get the response in same way. As we created the Gratitude exercise with the points to show gratefulness, we create the same to give Love to everyone and everything. Some of the common points in our life to show love should have been noted and most of the points in everyone are,

- ➤ I Love my Life.

- ➤ I Love my parents & my siblings.

- ➤ I Love my body.

- ➤ I Love the food and the water.

- ➤ I Love this beautiful Nature.

- ➤ I Love my friends and relatives.

- ➤ I Love the Money I own and will own.

- ➤ I Love the situations I'm in.

- ➤ I Love my work and I will get what I dreamt.

- ➤ I Love everything that is happening around me.

Depending in every individuals own life note the important things which gets involved in your daily life. Keep on showing love to all the creations around you, without your knowledge of change you will observe many things around you changing daily. You get happiness without knowing, you get confidence and strength for everything that will involve in your daily life that they will never leave your presence and they care you the more. For every handful of food you eat, water you drink, breath you take, emotions you feel etc., in everything where your presence is present you will find a better version of everything and that better one will bring you joy and happiness to your life. It all will happen only because you choose to care for things which are effective in your daily life and they start loving you more than normally they give you. Your thoughts will change things for you and your thoughts are one which brings anything you wanted to have in your life.

Love your time and the money. Don't misuse what you have now. If you start respecting them they'll come to you when there need for you is really important. These both have a larger impact in human life and many people run over them to make it stay with them. If you think you have needs, you find needs and if you don't you find none. This is what often happens but not with everyone. Know the real purpose of something and use what you have accordingly. Give love to all and don't expect anything in return.

The Power of Love

Love, it takes a human to any extend and also make a human to do anything. It gives you a lot of strength that whatever comes in between you will look smaller to get your love. Humans are created the way that they need a partner to share love and also to extend their family. But, love is not just a feeling to show only to partner or family, it is a feeling which brings tons of happiness to you if you start loving everything around you. One doesn't need to sacrifice their life to get things we needed, we just need to show love and gratitude towards everything.

First of all everything starts from us. We need to love ourselves the more first. It needed to be in a way which teaches us to spread love among everyone. We need to understand that everyone has same respect towards their life. This only thinking will change your behaviour. If you have known about what you wanted and what everyone wanted is same, you will definitely start to respect everyone. This happens only because you have love for yourself and you have knowledge that everyone will have the same towards themselves. If you change your way of thinking that not only you exist, but also everyone and the feelings are common to everyone, you automatically choose to show respect to the person beside you.

When you know it hurts you when you got a hit, you will also have known that someone who got hit also get hurt. When you know it makes you sad when someone laugh at you, you will also have known that someone whom you make laugh of will also feel sad. I wanted to say that it is same for everyone. The feelings are same in everyone, if they're unable to show you that, you simply leave that. You will receive it in another way but don't mind if you won't get it from someone whom you wanted to get from. Start loving and respect everyone. Respect yourself, be a real man and everything follows eventually.

To all the people who feel sad for their lives that they have nothing in life but it's just sorrow which is always beside them, it is because you are welcoming it every time. You attract more sadness when you are sad and what that brings to you? It keeps on bringing you more sadness if you keep on crying for whatever that is happening. Change your thoughts and improve your mindset to overcome from sadness faster.

Every human life is designed in the same way. Every life has the same ingredients in their body. Some people may be born disabled but with their thoughts they can overcome them also. No one is born clever, no one is born poor. Every human have the same brains and hearts then why not every life the same? The thoughts affect the life. How we think is what we are and our life will be the same and is been. Knowledge brings change and knowledge comes to one who keep finding ways to get knowledge but not to the one who doesn't obey their own parent's words. The saying "knowledge is Divine" is because it brings you everything. It teaches you everything. Always be ready to face any type of situation. Keep on chasing more knowledge, there's lots of knowledge present in this World. Even you know everything about earth and life, there's still more present to know every day and from everywhere.

To get anything you need to give something. Don't expect anything from anyone not even an introduction, but question yourself that if they won't, Why can't you? Let you be the first one to start anything. To start relations, to work, to help, to respect, to give etc., and without your notice you will make everything around you work for you, respect for you, care for you. Before questioning someone for anything first question yourself that are you ready to give the answer for the same question if asked. Never let someone question you or disrespect you. You keep on doing your own work and behave yourself politely with everyone the same whoever they may be, but with love and respect. To all the things and changes you want in your life, you get more than that without noticing. Try to learn and study everything carefully. Don't get over excited to solve things taking your knowledge as a chance. Be patience and mind your words while talking with someone. How much relation you may have with someone, no one wants themselves to be treated negatively. Think you being in those situations and behave everywhere.

Love brings you whatever you want, if it won't then the process of showing your love need to be changed. Love needed to be given or shown to someone you love depending on how they want to get loved. If you are expecting love from someone, you need to give it to them in the way in which they can feel it. You can't be quiet thinking you gave love and it'll return else it often returns when you are true. Gain knowledge about all the things to handle everything around you easily.

A never ending feeling

Spread peace and you will get peace following towards you. Love is not a small feeling to show only for some people or things. It is a never ending feeling that if you keep on loving, everything around you there will be keep on taking love from you for the many creations on Earth. There are plenty of creations in the planet, if not planet you can even love anything in the universe; the moon, the stars, the Sun. Expecting love from people may sometime disturb your whole mind because of the change in thoughts between people. Everyone has their own way of expressing love, what they know - they show. So, we can't force someone to love the way as we wanted to be loved. Simply it's better to love the things which are very important for us, from the clothes we wear to the vehicles we have to roam we can show love to everything. Love is not just a smallest creation, if you keep on digging it deeper you will be keeping on knowing more and new about love every day.

Food, water and shelter are the three things which every human being always strive to have with them constantly. Most of the people don't even respect the food they eat, the water they drink and the place they live. This happens only when we doesn't know the value for something. The things which we get easier will have no value, but for which we struggle we praise them. Everyone needed to remember that whatever they have now is a result for the struggle someone had faced in their family. In the same way, you be someone to get give more to your next generations or at least try to defend what you have. Wise people never choose to spoil the respect they have and will mostly care about everything.

Know about the different situations where other people are in, they maybe better or worse than you. You aim to be better than you have and maintain what you have with you now but don't let it fall to worse. Learn to realize the value of the things which you have every time for you in your life. You are one among the fewest percentage of life on earth if you are getting food every three times a day. Most of the people will have sleepless nights and many can't even find food twice a day. Feel happy that you are not among them and learn to start respecting food if you have anything to eat every day and also keep on giving respect to the people who feed your stomach working endlessly without quitting in any situation.

Keep on loving all these things and people which are very effective in your daily life. Many of the human beings don't care about most of common routine things which they have or get daily. But those things are common for you but not to all the living beings. What you have is because how you are. Your thoughts make your future and bring everything to you depending on that. Your respect and love towards everyone and everything tell their presence with you. Love is the only feeling which stays strong in every human mind and also between all the creations. Love is the only thing which can keep all the bonds alive even without wanting your presence. Learn loving and everything around you brings you lots of peace and happiness. Your love brings you what you desire. Love is not just a feeling to keep it aside but a feeling which always stay top among every emotion and attachment.

Our thoughts influence all the things around us. And when those thoughts have most of the love in it, then it will definitely make everything rise behind us as we wanted to become. Your love for everything impacts you to the many things you desire. It shows how strong you want something. If you are faking love towards someone or what you desire to get, the result will be the same as you do. Never ever play with the feelings, it will cost you more than you never expected to get. That will destroy everything even you have high thoughts in your mind. You won't be able to do anything without having peace with you. Happiness only can bring you more happiness. No person can smile with lots of pain in heart and that pain make all the things happen worse. So, never think about making others fool with the name of love. First think that you are affecting your own life before going to affect others. What you think you become, if you want to fool someone you are making yourself the fool first. Try to give the purest love and that will be returned to you.

Don't expect love from the same person or thing to whom you gave your love to, you will definitely get that love and care multiple times from the right person on the right time. Keep on giving love and spreading love among every creature and that keeps you all the things placed at the right time in your life.

Question yourself that what is the only thing that is affecting your life? What is the difference between others and you who are good in maintaining relations or who are happy with what they have in life. The first answer will be your thoughts and the second will be your care towards others. If you think of having something or someone in your life, you shift your thoughts to behave good with them and that will bring you what you want. In the same way if you want everyone and everything to care for you, it is you who must start loving them. If you show caring to someone you will get that in return unexpectedly. In life, if you have people to talk about you politely with others when you are not present, it is only because of your love which makes people talk about you truly. Your respect and behaviour towards them make those people to talk with others about you politely. After all you doesn't need to act to get respect, you just be genuine and make everything true from heart and it will all get returned to you in of your life.

If you keep on asking yourself that why are you not able to maintain any relation or the needs constantly with you, it all will be because of the love you have for them. If you keep on acting that you are giving love, those things also keep on moving far from you unnoticingly. Make anything in your life to stay constant in any type of situation. How worse the situation be people and needs should never leave you and that happens with your thoughts and love for them. You don't need to have any relationship with someone to behave properly with them, all you need is a kind heart. Let others be your relatives, friends or anyone you just need to behave kindly with everyone. You just need to keep on giving love and respect to others. If you get insulted or feel any bad feeling about anyone, don't even let those people to affect your mind and try to come back to normal as soon as possible. As your thoughts affect your life, your anger may make things fall worse around you. So always try to not lose your temper and pull back yourself when you feel disgusting or annoyed with any type of situation or people. Try to have peace all over your mind. As your thinking affect everything, think whatever happens with you that only bring good to you and that happens only for a good cause.

Nothing seems simpler unless you go for it. You don't need to take anything as harder or easier. Try to keep everything simpler. Don't make the tough one's easier and also don't make the easy one's get tougher for you. Take everything to be simple and the result will wonder you because you don't expect anything to show a change in your life from it. Always remember that this is one of an experience and this is not the end of the story. As you have a hope to wake tomorrow, also hope that something better is coming your way to change your whole life.

Respect & Emotions

There are many common things in every living being's and which gets attached to everyone are the emotions. Let that be love or hate it will definitely show impact in everyone's life. The thing is it all depends on the behaviour which others have or do our own selves which make to behave politely with others or not. It's all love that brings everyone together and makes every relation stay stronger. To the many people who feel they are not suitable for love it's because how they are and how the people or situations around them are. If they change their thoughts to love everyone and everything around them, the same love they show will also come back to them. Our attitude and behaviour with others tell everything about us. The more pride you feel about yourself, the more you are damaging your own identity. You may get identity if you are proud but that will be in the negative form. No one wants themselves to be identified negatively in the society. Everyone wants to be respected and want others to talk good about them. To make it happen, first you need to start loving and respecting all the things and people around you.

One's a person gets independent of their parents and stand on their own legs then the value of the respect and talking good about them becomes vital. What matters more to the most of the common people is respect. They will do anything to get respect and also go to any extend to maintain the respect others give to them. Respect is one of the important things in everyone's life who think there life is only about being in a good position and what other people think about them. Here, the main thing is people may respect you to the fear you create in them but they will definitely talk bad about you when you are not within them. You will only get true respect when you respect others wholeheartedly but not with fear. Love and respect are two things which have a difference but if you observe they are linked with each other. If you give love to someone, it means you are giving your time and feelings to others and that brings you respect. One's you start playing a key role in your house you'll be able to know the complete importance of the respect. Respect is never earned making someone fear rather it is earned winning the hearts of the people.

Smallest things bring the biggest changes in many people lives. The smallest lives don't need bigger things or biggest feelings from you, you first need to shower some love and that brings most of the happiness in their life. Your behaviour with others tells what type of a person you are and do you need to get respected or not. If you go to work somewhere or start doing business to earn money, you need to maintain healthy relations with people around you, this may not show more effect in jobs but in business you need to watch all your moves and words carefully. Depending on your words and how you behave with others people decide that they can purchase anything from you or not. Your patience, your attitude and your words describe your confidence on what you are selling and also make them to visit again. In jobs you spend most of your day in office only and if you won't keep on giving respect or helping others in need, there won't be anyone available to you when you want someone to get help. The small things show major impacts, so never underestimate anyone or anything with your thoughts and negligence.

When you are in true and deep love, you come to a belief that you can go to any extend to achieve your love. It brings you a feeling that you can win even you have many hurdles in your way. Love is a wonderful feeling which keeps on telling you that everything is possible and you have no limits in achieving your true love which may be with a person or a thing, if your love is true for it and you want it so hard it will definitely come to you. Our expectations are biggest spoilers in our life. Try to do something without any expectation and it'll definitely give you happiness because you never expected the result. Don't expect to get love from same rather be aware to notice how you are receiving it because you'll compulsory get what you have given.

As beautiful the love is, in the same way it also make humans not to do any work and pushes to just keep on loving whom they love. It also doesn't let us to assign any work to someone whom we love. Where there is true love there exists some fear, a fear which is because of a thought that they may lose whom they love. It is because that no one can resist if they lose someone whom they love deeply. This all happens because of the lack of confidence in you or maybe from whom you are getting loved. Build confidence and take everything to notice good things are coming your way.

One of the purest loves on this planet is which we get is from our parents, the love which they show is always endless and doesn't have any limits. You may have many people to cheer for your success but your parents are the only one who struggle with you to get you succeed. No one in this planet celebrate your important days with others like your parents do. They are the most selfless characters in everyone's life who doesn't want anything from you but just want your happy faces. I always keep on thinking the same question in my mind from people who had just lost their parents say that- I never came to know the importance of my parents when they were alive!! Why does someone only come to know the importance when they had lost something. It is because you are unable to notice what is happening around you, from whom you are getting love and from whom you are getting cheated. Question yourself that, why can't you love someone if the only reason for their life is you and your love.

Parents doesn't need anything from you, they just want you to get succeeded in your life. They'll only feel proud when you get succeed. The true love a person can get is from their parents. Your mother and father simply won't work there whole day even you are troubling them, that all happens because they completely find meaning of their life in making you a real man. Never hurt your parents and also don't regret after you don't have them for the same. What you have now only exists now. If a living being or a thing exists in your life, try to completely respect them. They simply won't come to you without any meaning. Any relation you have with someone or a thing is mostly because there is a purpose for the existence of it in their life or does in your life.

First of all learn to love everything you have and everyone who is there for you. Love your parents, your friends and your relatives. Don't waste your time in search of new things. Everything happen as it needed to be happened in your life. Keep on spreading love all over you that even if anyone hates you change it into love. It brings many changes in you- in the way you watch everything, in the way you do anything, in the way if you want something.

After you get habituated to loving for no cause, you would have been already gained lots of peace and happiness in your life. The one thing which always make a person unsatisfied with life is not money or people or property, it's because of no peace and happiness in their life even they earn plenty of money. There are many people who have everything which most of the people doesn't have but they will always be searching for happiness. There will be people who don't have what most of the people have but there will be happiness with whatever they have and whatever they do. It all depends in the way we deal with everything. The true meaning of life is to be happy and make everyone around us happier. If you have something which others don't, make them happier with what you have and if you are missing anything in your life, try to find it in others.

Emotions are really hard to understand and also in the same way they are easy to understand. In depends in the situations but they are powerful. They can convert anything to any extend or any extend to anywhere. Learn, experience and respect what you have with you in your life. Never disrespect or hate any creation. Don't remember the word hate in your life. Everything will change accordingly if you are positive. Change everything to be loved and start taking it from thereafter. Keep on loving yourself and spread it all over to see the magic of Love in your life.

Attitude

Attitude is the main thing which tells a lot of stories about everyone because attitude defines one's behaviour and that behaviour define everything about someone. Attitude depends in the way you think and that is what gets opened with your body language. Our body language is a simple replica of our mind. We can't judge others completely just with the body language to define what type of a person they are. But behaviour tells something more than what body language can't. So, the behaviour is important because it defines your way of thinking. Making your atmosphere positive is also an important thing to add power to your thoughts.

If others think bad about you that brings negativity and thus the thought power get affected. It is important to balance this and this happens with the change within you.

Our attitude can be described in two ways, the first way is which makes someone frighten by how we behave with others, this way gives disrespect and also may give negative impact's to others about us. The second way is which makes others come to us, to spend time with us because this doesn't make someone frightened and also they feel that they get respected depending on how we behave with them. Every person has these two options to tell how to behave with others and depending on their mindsets they choose their way of behaving. To get loved or to get hated, to get respected or to get disrespected, to get attention or to be unnoticed the choice depends on your thoughts. What you choose between all these opposites tell what your life is and what you are as a person.

If you start learning everything carefully you come to know that everyone wants to get noticed and everyone wants to get respected. A person only get respected and noticed when he has achieved something or did anything to the nation and its people or at least behaved politely with others. Your behaviour with others brings a good or a bad name to you and your family. Our attitude should never insult someone or should not make someone feel bad but rather make someone to come to us when they are in trouble. Someone only comes to you when you have a great attitude with them. Your attitude defines who you are and what you are. Your mindset, your character, your behaviour everything depends in your attitude. Besides, it is the only thing which keeps you high among all others. You have two choices the first one-which frightens and the second one-which respects. Choose what you want and how to behave with others and it brings what you give.

You need to point out the differences between what a real man is and what does someone who isn't true have. You need to know what makes someone give love to you and what makes someone hate you. What are those things which can have impact in your life if you want them to show positivity? What are those which can bring negativity in your life with the change in behaviour of the people? Knowledge is divine so does the character. What you choose will describe what needed to come to you.

Everything starts from our mind. Our thoughts make things work for us. What you think, you become. If you think of giving wrong to others, everything brings bad to you. If you think of giving right to others, everything brings good to you. So it all starts from you and within you. You don't have anyone to compete in your life. It's only you with whom you always compete. Your thoughts are which you always compete with. Thoughts are not easier to win, to take control of it and to make it work as how we wanted is not easier to converge it to our dream all the time.

Depending in a life's position there will be many unknown changes and connections between people which bring changes in minds. It is not just connections but also our likes, dislikes, unexpected movements etc, which all have impact in our mind. Between all of these things it is not easier to control our thoughts to think only about positivity. There will be many thoughts running along with the changes in time. Sometimes you lose focus, sometimes you lose confidence and all this will have impact in your thoughts.

It is very important to have a great focus on what we want to have in our life. Whatever may come, it should not impact on our dream. What may be the situation or whoever we meet we should not be going to take any chances in changes of getting success. The confidence should bring us positivity but not take us into bad atmosphere. You'll come to think like this when you have a good attitude. Your attitude tells about your mindset. How hard you try to reach your goal, what determination you have in your life will all be created with a better attitude. So it is important to have a great attitude and it gets built with the different experiences in life. That will define how strong you are in your life and how you will take the different challenges you get in your life. Remember to not give up easily on anything. It is the biggest thing one should always feed in their heads.

What more Attitude speaks

Most of the times our attitude gives us spirit to never give up easily on what we want to attain in our life. To all those things which we want in our life it's only our attitude which always keep on pushing us towards our dream. A good attitude is definitely needed which never says to give up our dream easily. Our attitude depicts how stubborn we are to get something we desire to have in our life. That is because many people say that 'Attitude is everything', it simply tells what kind of a human we are and what our capability is.

Every individual person wants to get well settled, to have a nice house, to have a nice family, to have a good income, to travel wherever they wish etc., most of the people dream this to have in their life, keeping this aside those who make them come true are the rarest between all the people who desire all of these things. What's the difference between the people who make this and who just dream about this? The difference is in the attitude of those who win and those who just dream. How our attitude is linked to our mindset is that- it tells how strong we are to get something we dream, how badly we want something we desire, how strong we are and up to how much extent we can go to achieve our goal. Our attitude changes our mindset and it shows the impact in our thoughts. Everything is interlinked so it is necessary to maintain consistent in creating positive vibrations and a never give up attitude.

Every person have dreams, have wishes but those who make them to have in their life in reality and bring them in their life for real are the one who want them so hardly. They can do whatever to gain it and that is what makes them special from all the people and it is what which let them attain what they dream to have in their life. Attitude tells about your mindset that is why everything in your mind gets reflected with your body language. If you are proud of something it gets projected in your attitude, if you are happy it gets projected in your attitude, if you are anger, sad, jealous, merciful etc all these emotions which will be in the mind gets reflected with our attitude and that is why attitude defines our mindsets. A person can tell what's running in your mind by the way you walk or the way you are behaving with others or even with your body language. So many things depend in Attitude.

It is not easier to maintain consistent, to keep consistency it take a lot of hard work. Your dedication play important role and sometimes you may need to leave your favourite things to maintain consistency. If you want to become an athlete, you need to focus mainly in your body. Food is important in maintaining body structure and those who choose sports in their life need to leave many favourite foods for their body's growth. Depending in different goals you have to neglect those which were important for you. If you need to work on your goal, you need to spend more time in researching about it and also to gain knowledge in the field you choose.

To work for growth in life you should leave all those to which you got habituated. I think cricket or any games are a real emotion to many of the people, spending time in TV, indoor games, family discussions etc, all these things will be given less importance and also they disturb our mind sometimes. A positive attitude keeps us far from all these things. What we needed is important for us now to change our life. It is not wrong to support others but first of all you should create space in your life to make yourself settled in something. No one listen's you if you haven't made anything in your life. You or your words will only be respected when you are in a certain position. Don't give a chance to let others talk about you. Build yourself and everyone will automatically listens your answers.

The same happen in everyone's life and it is all about importance which results. To dream and make it come true or to let it be a dream only depends in what you choose. You only get satisfied with your life if you have your dreams fulfilled. To get your dreams achieved you need to have strength in your mind, the stronger your mindset is, the stronger your attitude will be and it shows you the way to your destination.

Time brings a lot of changes in your life, it brings lots of happiness at a time and opposite to it in the same time. We can never be the same as we used to do always. We get many ups and downs in our life but we can only resist all of them when we have capability to deal with everything the same. Life is all about experiencing what is happening with our daily life. They are common and the way you take them defines how matured you are in your life.

Maturity deals with how we think of some situation which may or may not be in our favour.

Maturity is something which changes with the knowledge, experiences and with the growth of life. That is the thing which will keeps you high and also low among many people depending in how you treat the situations. When you are positive you take everything in the same and it will have a good impact in everyone, also the bad impact happens when you are negative. Whatever you choose to define a life, it takes how your thoughts are. Thinking has much ability and so everything starts through our mindset. The better mindset gives the better result and so does bring the positive changes you needed in your life.

The best passage I saw!!

Everything- the good and bad, pleasure and pain, approval and disapproval, achievements and mistakes, fame and shame all come and go. Everything has a beginning and an ending and that is the way it is supposed to be.

Every experience you have ever had is over. Every thought you've ever had started will finished. Every emotion and mood you've experienced has been replaced by another. You've been happy, sad, jealous, depressed, anger, in love, shamed, proud and every other conceivable human feeling. Where did they all go? The answer is no one really knows. All we know is that, eventually, everything comes and goes.

Our disappointment comes about essentially two ways. When we are experiencing pleasure- we want it to last more. Or when we are experiencing pain- we want it to go away, now. It actually doesn't. When something is happening that we enjoy, know that it is wonderful to experience the happiness it brings and it eventually pass. If you are experiencing some displeasure or pain, know that this too shall pass. Keeping this awareness close to your heart is a wonderful way to maintain your perspective even in the face of adversity. One must tolerate this appearances and disappearances of non-permanent emotions without being disturbed.

Don't let your mind to take over those appearances and disappearances of these non-permanent emotions. Pleasure and pain may be completely different and give you different results but one who is having impact with them is you. It is only you who need to have control over them. How you take them or deal with them defines what you think. It is not simple but you need to take it simple to practice it. Nothing comes in the first day, you need to gain grip over the situations to get habituated to it. So, now you need to start dealing with situations to not let them show impact on you.

Be prepared for the worst but don't make the worst to get habituated. Don't prepare for easier things and also don't take anything which comes without any effort towards you. You will only know the real meaning of something when you struggle for it. That effort gives you happiness and so you can enjoy whatever you have as a result. This result won't last and it is just an experience in your life. Whatever you go through your life are just the experiences you will have so don't think of anything that it will lasts with you. Nothing lasts permanent and also you.

Dealing with problems!!

Life is not only meant for pleasures you enjoy but also the pain you experience. Problems are common in everyone's life, as the problems arises there are also solutions to every problem. As we think we become, we always need to be positive to get solutions for the problems which disturb our minds. The more negative we think the more worst the situation will becomes. When problems arises we open up all the chances to get our problem solved, in that case sometimes we will be unable to decide what is correct and what is wrong and it all depends upon how we think every time. If our mind is not in our control then the situation may become worse. If we are habituated to be calm and composed we can make things happen better.

No one can control their temper if they are in critical situations but there should be one thing to remember every time that we are creating mess in our own life. Critical the situations, critical our chances become. It is never easy to hold sadness or pain when we see our loved ones in trouble or worst situations. Remember only one thing that those who are born need to die definitely. Everyone will face good times, bad times, pleasures, adversity and death and that is what life is all about. We come alone and we go alone, keeping this in mind try to mostly hold everything.

Emotions are which make people to do anything. You can also be easily fooled with the emotions you have. It happens more often when you have true belief and love for someone. It is not compulsory to leave your emotions and also not compulsory to give it more specification. Nothing hurts more than those who hurt us being with us every time but learn to not give them that chance. Be prepared for something more than what it needs on an average.

Don't give more importance to the new situations. If you think of now your past existence may get changed with it also sometimes you need to change when you have bad existence with you in the past. Change is good sometimes and also sometimes it may affect but you need to defend both of them. You need to defend yourself and the people who follow your way. You should not be keep on imagining that should had one or this should have done, what done is done you can't change it. Move with what it teaches you and bring the change to your present. The change always will have impact but it also won't stay longer, whatever it may be that won't stay. Create better experiences and keep on using them to make the better happen to you in your life. A great ability is all needed to understand all these things and it also eventually happen with the growth you want to have in your life.

A Champion's Mind...

What is the sole difference between a winner and the loser is the way they think. Only a winner knows what the struggle is and a loser is someone who doesn't try seeing the process of the struggle. No one wants to know about the struggle, everyone simply denote is they are born lucky to reach there. Most of the people don't even try to think to reach great destinations in life. It is all because of the fear which is continuing from ages.

One needed to simply believe that they're going to win what the process may be. The thoughts make your way and your strength declares you are going to win or lose. Whatever the result be, learn something from it. This is not the end and this is not the only thing which is important to you. The lesson you learned here may help you in some other situation. Winners are one who keeps focus in learning and gaining knowledge. Losers are one who give up with the critics and start to criticise others with their experience. So, it is not necessary to give importance to all the people who talk about you and criticise you. If you have a great attitude you will use that to add more strength than you normally have.

The champion is someone who has the ability to win. Even the process should feel proud of your struggle to the attitude you have towards winning. Champion is someone who can hold any type of situations without any fear and any changes will also doesn't impact. A champion wins not because of luck or something, they win because of their hard work and the ability they have in them. They win with their thought power which has complete strength in everything of success.

Attitude is everything because it is what builds what needed when we doesn't have any power to move forward. A great attitude is a way to a great life. Have a better attitude to respect everyone and stand to bring change in the people around you.

Meditation

The meaning of the Dhyana yoga (meditation) has mostly become a task in everyone's life. But the real purpose of the meditation is needed to be one among the main necessity like food, water and air. Meditation is not something which just purifies your body but it is the work which purifies your whole life. Meditation is a greatest skill which will teach you many interesting things about nature and life. It is something which mainly works on your concentration to help you improve the natural abilities. Many of the people who are not able to concentrate mainly on what they want will be because of the fluctuations which mind creates. With the power of meditation it can all be recalled and can make someone more focussed. Meditation in not something to perform 5 to 10 minutes concentrating in forcing breath or chanting any God's name as many teach, it is about concentrating the breath we take without forcing it.

Meditation is concentrating in breath. The knowledge in breath is called the knowledge in meditation. When you have knowledge about breath you have complete knowledge about meditation. What is necessary to a human for a complete living is breath and knowledge. If you know completely about breath you already know half of your life clearly. So, it is very necessary for everyone to know about meditation and to spread about meditation. It brings awareness in people about breathing ways making everyone's life better and the better life starts with the better works you prefer to do in your life.

Every individual person has time and energy until some age on an average in everyone's life. It is the time which defines the remaining life in a person. To the energy we have, meditation adds more energy to what is actually present.

Children's needed to have more energy to the time they spend in playing. The children's age is the age where humans start learning new behaviours. What to do and what not to do throughout the complete life will starts from childhood. It is the age where everything starts and hence it is better to teach meditation from childhood, hence it will become a habit in everyone's life and it will add more energy and patience for everyone.

Among different arts and studies, Dhyana kala & Dhyana vidya are the important one and the most essential one. Why is this have that much of specification is because it is what something which changes all the things in a daily life. It is what brings confidence, positivity, strength etc. What more do you need in life to make it better than the knowledge of breathing. That is why it is specified to be top among all other studies and this will be totally in the hands of parents to teach their children with the better knowledge, to create positivity in the negative things and also to be confident every time.

There will be an interrelation between breath and heart. And breath is the only thing which is connected between heart and our body. That is why the changes in breath changes heart condition. If breath is low, heart will get low and if it is high, heart will go high .So maintaining breath, maintains heart and our life is in the breath. Our heart is only related to breath and it gets better only by getting good breath. This can be possible through meditation because meditation is concentrating in breath. It doesn't gets better even you chant 1000's of mantra's every day. It may lead in losing life but it doesn't even help to build energy in your life. We waste lot of energy in watching, talking, listening, thinking etc. First of all we need to save all of that energy. If we are able to save all the energy we lose everyday by all these activities, we can use it in making our life better with meditation.

Meditation is not about chanting mantras, Meditation is not possible if your eyes are open and it is not at all meditation. It should be done by joining your two hands and bringing legs together. You can sit however you want and your position doesn't change any energy levels.

Closing your eyes brings you much energy and it also stops your energy from getting wasted. The difference between silence and meditation is meditation gets energy whereas silence transfers the energy. Our breaths have comic energy in it which is the main cause for living. As we can't see current in a wire but make things work, we also can't see that cosmic energy but it does its work and your living is an example for that.

To make meditation a daily habit, everyone should follow the meditation doing activity for 41 days depending on the age you have. If you are 10 years old meditate for a minimum of 10 minutes daily. Do meditation two times a day so you can bring better growth in life. As we talked it takes 41 days to make something a habit in our life.

No teacher, No guardian, No parent can bring the energy in your life until you start behaving yourself. It is only you who can change your life. You should never reduce the minimum meditating time. You can extend your time but should never reduce it to get better results. You will only get better if you concentrate or spend more time in something and from now make meditation a habit. Learning about meditation and teaching it will be a great cause in life. Reading books related to the spirituality brings more Scope in life and also helps in better understanding.

Meditation is not related to any religion or country. It is a science and it is a basic common sense. Every human needs breath and knowing about it is very essential. Small knowledge about breath brings big changes in your life. The use of medicines and doctors has become very important in everyone's life. It is all because of the changes in our strengths and atmosphere and this all can be reduced with the power of meditation. There will be no need of any medicine & doctor if you can control your breath and this will only happen with the knowledge in meditation. This also helps in bringing good habits, keeping bad habits far away from everyone. Good habits and good behaviour bring much good to you and helps in building good life. So, it is very necessary to know about meditation and also to bring awareness in the people by spreading about the power and knowledge about meditation. Good people make good community and it bring more happiness.

The more knowledge you get about meditation, the more time you will spend in doing this meditation perfectly, the more good you can bring in your life. If it is hard to meditate or you are unable to believe the power of meditation, first try it one's. It is always better to take a chance and try something new. If you try this then only you will know about this. With words there is nothing going to get changed, you need to experience everything in actions and this will definitely be liked by everyone.

Meditation is a way to bring spiritual consciousness to your life. Spirituality is something which brings you peace and so does the happiness. It is not something which tells you to leave all your relations and spend your life in monkhood, rather it is something which makes your life meaningful with the knowledge you get in the way of spiritual process. You will come to know much knowledge related to the human life with spirituality and it tells the real destination to your life. Everyone prefers to know the knowledge about the human life and everyone needs to make it worthy.

You will know the real value of this human life when you prefer something which teaches you in detail about this topic. Being spiritual brings you this knowledge about life and it moulds you to live the best. It never tells you to leave anything you are having now rather it adds many new things in your life. It is also something which can make you a real human being with the knowledge it teaches you in search of the purpose to this life. It is one among a way to make your thoughts powerful.

Learning Meditation

It is not easier to make something a new habit to our routine life. It takes a great mindset to be dedicated and also it needs more integrity to schedule to make something a habit if you are in any profession. The time someone makes to get habituated depends in the thinking & the knowledge you have for something. It takes nearly 41 days to make any new thing a habit in everyone's life. So, let everyone try meditation for 41 days with the minimum time and you can see results within 41 days by yourself in your behaviour and the way you think.

Concentrating in breath is not an easy task. Many may think it will be easier to learn breathing with meditation. Forceful breath or chanting mantras with eyes closed is an easier task but not concentrating in breath. The concentration in breath takes your complete mind power to observe the inhaling and exhaling of air in our body. It is not something which creates sound. Meditation doesn't create any sound and also sound disturbs meditation. Meditation is needed to be done heart fully then only it improves your ability.

To concentrate in your breathing first of all you need is to control your thoughts. You should not let any thoughts disturb you or you should not think about anything while meditating. Meditation brings you cosmic energy with the concentration you make in your breathing. It takes practice to gain cosmic energy and to sense the flowing of energy to your body. Nothing is easier to get until you practice to make it a habit. The more practice you make on anything, the more high positions you reach in it depending with the knowledge on the subject.

Meditation also has different positions and who try to learn meditation are the beginners in the path of meditating. It takes time for anything to gain more knowledge in something. Even if anyone try to tell, you can't understand it for the position you are in. So, be patient to learn and practice meditation more. You will have better results in your life and it will make you control your thinking.

Our thoughts are the main root in our life. What we think to do now or choose now will change our future. So, the thoughts we have will have everything about our future. Positive thoughts make life positive without any worries and they are all very necessary for everyone. The way we speak, we talk, we do all depends in the way we think. It is also necessary to convert negative situations or ideas into positives and it is not easy without having better knowledge about handling situations and meditation helps in all of these things without knowing. We are the own creators of our present and let build it better, at least happier.

We create our destiny and it depends in what we choose among different ways we have to get choose. Visualisations are important in life and one can't visualise better if you have negative thoughts in mind. Visualizing something needs better understanding about how they work. It is a concept which needs our complete emotions to make something come true. They do play a vital role in bringing something you desired to have in your life. It is all in the knowledge we gain throughout the times we spend in our life. Everyone need to know what are those things which will play an important role in making something we desire to come true in our life.

First among everything it takes a small thought to make us believe that we will have it. That small thought will give you lots of spirit when you will be completely exhausted with the process you were in. Later on you will go through different experiences your life teaches you. In this you build many new things, many new schedules, many thoughts etc, also you will lose many favourites, many people, many thoughts etc, your thoughts will be keep on changing and those only give you or make you the strength you needed. Your mind is everything, your thoughts are everything. They always needed to be fed with more dedication than before.

So, it is essential to make mind to our control and everything follows that eventually. Positivity is what needed for everyone and it brings Hope in any type of situation you are facing. It is about the knowledge someone have which tell you to choose the directions between the good and the bad also between the positives and the negatives. And there lies everything-respect, discipline, manners, honour and mostly the meaning of life and the type of people who we have supporting us.

One thing is always important for everyone and that is because we are a part of it. We are a part of this Nature and it will only support you when you are supporting it. Meditation is one among a part which links you with the nature and it will all take care of you with the way you think and act accordingly. Thinking good makes in being good and brings only good that it is what nature expects. So, always be friendly with everyone and everything, if you won't get love or respect from them, nature will provide it in different forms and will compulsory brings you what you are giving. Spread love, Spread meditation and this brings more joy and happiness in the atmosphere around you.

The Conclusion

The life of a human has a specification. You are born as a human for a reason. You need to use the complete power which only a human life will have. Think of being in a state of other creations than human being then you'll know that you have better abilities than them. You have a lot of capability in yourself. The mind, the body, the character, everything is a blessing which only a human being can have. Know your ability and use it completely to make it purposeful. Get the knowledge of life. Nothing happens without any reason. Don't ever underestimate yourself in any situation. Try and try but don't fail to try. Enjoy the process.

Nothing stays permanent so does the human life also. Make friends but not enemies. Love but not hate. Learn but not neglect. Spread love and it will get returned to you. The happy faces you make will be the happy situations you get. Make your life habituated to keep everything simple. Use your complete Thought Power. BE GRATEFUL, NEVER GIVE UP & LOVE YOUR LIFE.

9 789356 210325